# "THE HIGHEST PRAISE OF GALLANTRY"

THE

# MEMORIALS

OF

DAVID T. JENKINS

AND

JAMES E. JENKINS

# MEMORIALS

OF

# DAVID T. JENKINS

AND

# JAMES E. JENKINS

---

UTICA, N. Y.

T. J. GRIFFITHS, PRINTER, EXCHANGE BUILDINGS

1889

SCHROEDER PUBLICATIONS
2001

ISBN: 1-889246-17-4

**Cover:** (Left) David T. Jenkins, Colonel, 146th New York Volunteer Infantry (Fifth Oneida) was killed at the Battle of the Wilderness on May 5, 1864. His body was never recovered. (Patrick A. Schroeder Collection) (Right) James E. Jenkins, Captain, 146th New York Volunteer Infantry (Fifth Oneida) and the Oneida Cavalry. (Ann H. Ford Collection)

**Back Cover:** A striking albumen photograph showing four members of the 146th New York Zouaves taken in the fall of 1863 at Elmira, New York, where all four men were assigned to duty at the conscript depot. From left to right are David W. Allen, Chauncey B. Smith, Jesse C. Johnson, and John Duckworth. Of these, only Allen and Duckworth survived the war. Smith and Johnson were both captured at the Battle of the Wilderness. Smith was shot and killed by a guard while a prisoner of war, and Johnson succumbed to chronic diarrhea at Salisbury Prison in North Carolina. (Hendrick Hudson DAR Collection)

**Cover Design:** By Maria Ann Dorsett Schroeder

Printed by Farmville Printing
Farmville, Virginia

SCHROEDER PUBLICATIONS
12 Camellia Drive
Daleville, Virginia 24083
www.civilwar-books.com
civilwarbooks@yahoo.com

# FOREWORD

While researching materials for other books, including a reprint of *Campaigns of the 146th Regiment New York State Volunteers* by Mary G. Brainard (Schroeder Publications 2000), I discovered a little known memorial volume dedicated to two brothers who served in that distinguished regiment–David T. and James E. Jenkins. Not only did they serve with the unit, but David became colonel of this hard-fighting outfit, and James commanded Company H. Sadly, one of these brothers from Vernon in Oneida County, perished on the field of battle.

David, a 26-year-old lawyer and a skilled engineer who had graduated from Rensselear Polytechnic Institute, helped recruit the 117th New York Infantry (Fourth Oneida), before taking the field as a first lieutenant and adjutant of the 146th New York Volunteer Infantry (Fifth Oneida). He quickly jumped to the rank of major, then lieutenant colonel, and took charge of the regiment upon the promotion of Colonel Kenner Garrard. David commanded a brigade for a time in the winter of 1863-64,and displayed a talent for leadership and administration in theat responsible position. Leading the Zouaves of the 146th in a desperate charge at Saunders Field at the Battle of the Wilderness on May 5, 1864, he was twice wounded–once in the head and once in the body. The last that was ever seen of him, he was holding himself up with his sword and encouraging his men. He disappeared amidst the smoke and fury of battle, and his body was never recovered.

James Jenkins was a 20-year-old Hamilton College student when the war began. He left his classes and to become an officer in the Oneida Cavalry–an independent company that had the distinguished honor of being posted to the headquarters guard of the Army of the Potomac. On March 1, 1863, James transferred to the 146th New York and was wounded in the neck by a sharpshooter while the regiment occupied Little Round Top at Gettysburg, on July 2, 1863. After James mustered out, late in 1864, he returned to the Oneida Cavalry in January 1865, as its commander, and served to the end of the war.

The original printing of this book came about largely through the efforts of A. Pierson Case, who at age 44, mustered-in as a first lieutenant and quartermaster of the 146th. He personally knew the Jenkins boys and thought as much of them as they did of him. Not only does he pay tribute to his departed gallant friends, he gives an informative and concise history of the 146th, replete with anecdotes, that makes for entertaining reading. The memorials, written to eulogize the Jenkins brothers, tender ample tribute to their patriotic nature. This reprint will ensure that their sacrifices and courageous exploits will not be forgotten. These two soldiers deserved "the highest praise of gallantry."

Since the reprinting of the regimental history of the 146th which included 154 previously unpublished photographs, several more images of soldiers and veterans belonging to that regiment have come to light, some of which are now included in this volume.

Patrick A. Schroeder

Patrick A. Schroeder

**DAVID TUTTLE JENKINS**

After assisting to raise the 117th New York Infantry (Fourth Oneida), Jenkins was mustered in as a first lieutenant and regimental adjutant of the 146th on Aug. 26, 1862. Born May 4, 1836, the tall and slender 26-year-old had attended Rensselaer Polytechnic Institute in Troy, and was practicing law in Vernon at the commencement of the war. A competent soldier and skilled engineer, Jenkins was promoted major on Sept. 17, 1862, then to lieutenant colonel on July 23, 1863. On May 5, 1864, he was in command of the division pickets, but learning that an attack was to be made, he asked to be returned to his regiment to lead it into battle. At the head of the regiment he led his men in the charge across Saunders Field in support of the 140th New York. The last time he was seen by members of the unit, he had his back against a tree and was leaning on his sword. He had been wounded at least twice—once in the head and another shot through the body, yet he encouraged his men to "go on." Hopes that Jenkins had been captured faded as time passed. His body was never recovered. Major A. Pierson Case of the regiment remembered: "In a time of heroes, he too was a hero—he was ours, and we ought to be proud of him." This photo was taken by Brady in New York City. (Ann Ford Collection)

# TRIBUTES TO THE MEMORY

## --OF--

# Colonel David Tuttle Jenkins

---

*From the Utica Morning Herald, July, 1864.*

Among the long list of brave and true martyrs to our cause, who fell in the late battles, is reported the name of Col. David T. Jenkins, son of the late J. Whipple Jenkins, Esq., of Vernon, and a resident of that town. When it was proposed to raise the 146$^{th}$ he was appointed Adjutant by the recommendation of the war committees of the county; and from that time until its organization labored with unflagging zeal, and to more purpose than any other man, to make the regiment what it was. Previously he had been very efficient in stirring up and keeping active the war spirit of the county, and his appointment gave general satisfaction. On the organization of the 146$^{th}$ he was promoted to Lieutenant Colonel at the request of Col. Garrard, who saw in him eminent fitness for a military leader. When Col. Garrard was appointed Brigadier, he rose to the rank which he held at the time of his death. He was unacquainted with the science of arms when he entered upon his military career, but industrious study, added to a clear, ready and comprehensive mind, soon made him the equal of most, and superior of many, of the volunteer officers of similar rank, and the testimony in the army is that he was a most excellent officer. He participated, always bravely, in the great battles of Fredericksburg, Chancellorsville, and Gettysburg, and now leaves behind him an undying record. Col. Jenkins

Col. David T. Jenkins (left), General Spaulding (50th N. Y. Engineers), and Capt. James E. Jenkins (right) at Headquarters of Gen. Spaulding, Warrenton Junction, Va., Spring of 1864

was about twenty-eight years of age. He was one of the best surveyors in the county, and previous to joining the army had entered upon a promising practice as a lawyer. His brother, Capt. James E. Jenkins, also belongs to the 146$^{th}$, and it is hoped is still alive; and a mother, sister and brother are in Vernon. They will received hearty and widespread sympathy in their affliction.

---

*To the Editor of the Utica Morning Herald:*

As a friend and acquaintance of our lamented Col. David T. Jenkins, I wish to say a few words in memoriam of one so truly good and noble. So general is the sorrow for the loss of friends who have fallen in their country's cause, and so many have been the precious sacrifices, that individual losses seem to have been, as it were, swallowed up in the great general sorrow. But should it be thus? and should we forget to chronicle the noble lives–though all too short and fitful–of those whose example might well serve as models and towards whom we cannot feel too deeply grateful?

Colonel Jenkins was born in the year 1836 in the neighboring town of Vernon. From his earliest boyhood he was a model scholar, a youth of fairest promise. The boy was just merging into the man, when by the death of his father, he was left the counselor of his widowed mother, and the oldest of a family of three sons and a daughter. And well did he fulfil his trust, yielding tempting fields of enterprise in the West and elsewhere, to remain with them in the quiet village of his birth. He was everything that a son and brother could be. A lawyer by profession, he had a particular talent for engineering and surveying, and as a surveyor of the very first talent he was well known here. Few men in the country promised to be more useful or eminent in their profession than he, but his country called and early he went into the service as Adjutant. Soon he was promoted to Major, then to Colonel, and was an acting Brigadier for some months before his death. At the battle of Gettysburg, he won the highest praise of gallantry, being in a very exposed position. Of quiet and unpretending disposition, he was the best loved by those who knew him most intimately. Pure and irreproachable

**ROMEYN BECK AYRES**

Ayres was born in Montgomery County, New York, in December 1825. He graduated from the Military Academy at West Point in 1847, and did garrison duty in Mexico after the end of hostilities in the Mexican War. At the start of the Civil War, he was a captain in command of a battery of the 5th US Artillery and was present at the Battle of First Manassas. Ayres rose to the rank of brevet major general. In 1864-65, he had charge of the brigade, then the division in which the 146th New York served. He died December 4, 1888. (MOLLUS and the USAMHI)

in his character, his friendships were strong and true, and we who saw him at home last spring in the strength of manhood, little could realize that his noble form would so soon be laid low. It was in the fearful battle of the Wilderness he fell. The last that was seen of him he stood with his back against a tree, leaning on his sword, a bullet wound in his body and another in his head, and calling to his men to "go on." How long he lived is not known, save by Him to whose ever watchful care we can well leave him, believing that He did not permit him to suffer above which he was able to bear, and has regarded his martyr spirit with a crown of life.

A. V. E.
Utica, July 19th, 1864.

---

*Extract from a Letter to the mother of Col. Jenkins, from Maj. Gen. R. B. Ayers, U.S .A.*

Colonel Jenkins was in my command when he was killed in the battle of the Wilderness, May 5th, 1864. He was in command of the picket line of the 5th Corps that day, and requested me to relieve him, and let him take command of his regiment in the battle then imminent. That request was granted, and he commanded gallantly till he was killed. I had known him over a year, and I regarded him as one of the first and most promising officers in our armies. The country met with a great loss in his fall; his family, with an irreparable one. He was endeared to the whole division, and to all who knew him in the Army of the Potomac.

I am glad, madam, to send you this poor tribute from one who admired your gallant son.

Yours, very sincerely,
R. B. Ayers,
Maj. Gen'l U.S. Army.

---

# IN MEMORIAM

Killed in the battle of the Wilderness, May 5$^{th}$, Col. David Tuttle Jenkins of Vernon, Oneida Co., New York. Alas! how much of the great history of disappointed hopes, worth ambition, tender affection, deep sorrow, and unspeakable grief may be compressed in the record of a single sentence. In the loss of colonel Jenkins one more offering has been sacrificed on the costly altar of patriotism, a career of bright young promise closed, a sphere of active usefulness terminated, a source of influence in the community where he had been known from childhood, and had grown into a respected manhood, cut off, and a home bereaved of one in whom all the domestic affections were strong, deep, and fervent.

The father of Col. Jenkins, the late J. Whipple Jenkins, Esq., died in Vernon, in 1852. David, then a lad, grew up into the father's place in the family, and gradually was coming to fill it in the community. Having received a partial course of scientific instruction in the Rensselaer Polytechnic Institute, in Troy, he left that institution after an illness which rendered his health insufficient for its severe course of study, and prepared himself for entrance on his father's profession, the law. In this profession he was attaining a respectable rank, and acquiring a sound and increasing influence, when the war made its appeal to the patriotism of all classes and ages. Conservative in the constitution on his mind, educated from childhood in the traditions of the Democratic party, of which his father was a disciple and leader, protesting in his heart against the ultralism of both parties, this young, rising lawyer, with many ties, influences, comforts and prospects in the future that ordinarily bind one to home life, sedate in character, quiet in habits, fond of country life and satisfied in its pursuits, felt a moving power deeper than all these, and with chastened and sober views from solemn convictions of duty to country and the dearest interests of home, involved in the preservation of institutions which constitute all that is most valuable in country itself, parted from the endearing ties and relinquished the solemn responsibility of home, and gave himself henceforth to the defense of those institutions, and of the dear old flag which is the symbol of their glory.

This, it is true, is no isolated case. It is but one history out of the thousands of noble and brave young men, the good sons, the loved brothers, the endeared friends, who in giving themselves to their country, have passed out of our earthly homes and will be no more known in the places of influence in our communities. Why, then, pause to commemorate this instance of personal loss? Because, we answer, so many hears have throbbed with the same painful experience, and the word of commemoration that is soothing to one bereaved circle finds a response in the sympathies of hundreds of others. Besides, here was a young man of more than ordinary worth, of more than average ability, of culture, of solid qualities and of commanding influence; and it is due alike to the living and the dead that such should be honored in a grateful remembrance. In life honors worthily bestowed rapidly accumulated upon this young man. Appointed, first, Adjutant in the One Hundred and Forty-sixth Regiment of New York Volunteers, under the command of Col. Garrard, then recently from the command at West Point, under the eye of this experienced officer of the regular army, he was promoted to the post of Major, then Lieutenant Colonel, still under Col. Garrard, and when that officer was appointed to another field, his young subordinate succeeded to his rank and command.

Colonel Jenkins went with his regiment into that terrible battle of the Wilderness, never to return. His friends clung to the hope that he might be a prisoner until after long weeks of anxiety, the certainty of his death came to the dear home circle and there was no longer any hope. No hope did we say? Yes, there is one hope equal to even this terrible emergency that only can support and soothe the stricken hearts of the bereaved ones in the dear old home from whence the props and hopes and joys have gone out never to return; and that is one full of immortality–the gift of our Savior Jesus Christ.

Come, precious gift, to all these bereaved ones! Come in peace, in trust, in a reverent, unshaken confidence in God, in Christ, in His gospel of divine, truth, and in the immortal life it has revealed!

Rev. H. Emmons,
In "Washington National Intelligencer"

**KENNER GARRARD**

Born in Kentucky in 1827, Garrard attended Harvard for a year before leaving to enter West Point where he graduated eighth in the class of 1851. Captured by Texas insurgents on Apr. 12, 1861, and paroled. He served as commandant at West Point until appointed colonel of the 146th. Garrard brought discipline and military efficiency to the regiment. Garrard led the regiment at Fredericksburg, Chancellorsville, and Gettysburg. There, upon the death of Brig. Gen. Stephen H. Weed, he succeeded to the command of the brigade. He was promoted July 23, 1863, to brigadier general of volunteers. He commanded the brigade along the Rappahannock River, until put in charge of the cavalry bureau in Washington, DC. Garrard led a division of cavalry during the Atlanta Campaign, then a division of infantry in the 16th Corps during the Battle of Nashville. He took a major role in the capture of Mobile on Mar. 13, 1865, and received the brevet rank of brigadier and major general in the Regular Army. He resigned his commission on Nov. 9, 1866. Garrard died May 15, 1879, and was buried at Spring Grove Cemetery in Cincinnati, OH. Alfred Palmer wrote of his former commander: "to him much is due for the discipline and efficiency [of the regiment] . . . . He was a thorough soldier. A gallant officer, loyal, fearless & true and beloved by all his men." (Donald Wisnoski Collection)

# MEMOIR OF COL. DAVID T. JENKINS

*In his connection with the 146th N. Y. Vols., as delivered. at Vernon, N. Y., on Decoration Day, 1878.*

In August, 1862, David Tuttle Jenkins was sworn into the military service of the United States as Adjutant of a new regiment from Oneida County, known then as the Fifth Oneida.

A brief statement of the circumstances that led to this step, will help to define the position and character of the subject of this sketch.

The large call for troops in the summer of 1862 had seemingly about exhausted the voluntary enlistments in Oneida County. The members of the war committee of the county had been very active in their duties, and had called to their assistance influential citizens in every town. A fair record of the efforts of these men to fill the quota of the county–their persistent work, for many months, in organizing war meetings, and by addresses and extensive correspondence to fully arouse the patriotism of the people of the county–if such a record was possible--would show a vast amount of labor, and efficient management, the results of which justified the efforts. Prominent among the workers in this part of the county was David T. Jenkins. Three regiments largely made up from this county had gone forward when the formation of the fourth, and, as then thought, the last, was undertaken.

This was the 117$^{th}$.

No previous regiment hand so large and enthusiastic representation from this town.

About fifty of the stalwart young men of the town joined that regiment–most of them in the company of Capt. Geo. W. Brigham, who met his fatal bullet at Drury's Bluff, waving his hat to his men as he fell, and shouting, "Go on, boys, and give it to them!"

But when the 1,020 men of that regiment had left Rome, and word came from Albany that Oneida County was still short of her quota by one regiment, it did seem an almost impossible task to raise another thousand men. But the efforts never ceased or faltered. Col. Jenkins, then a quiet civil engineer, and the main stay of a widowed mother and younger brother and a sister, was one of the first to step forward with new methods and plans. He already felt ashamed of a longer stay at

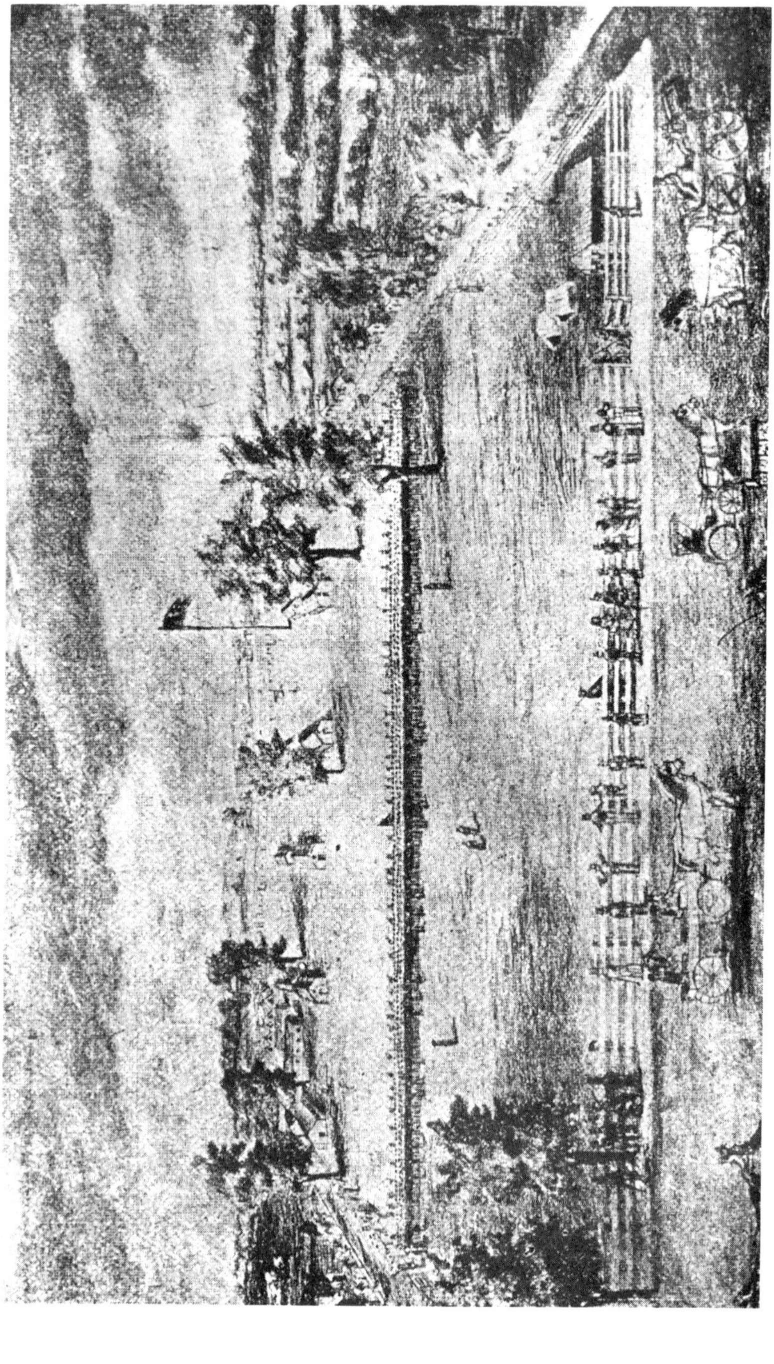

The Historic Camp Huntington at Rome, N. Y., as it Appeared in 1862

From a pen sketch by F. S. Honsinger

Here the One Hundred and Forty-sixth Regiment drilled, preparing for war

home and of saying to others "Go!" Now was the time to say "Come." But notwithstanding these new efforts, recruiting in this town went on slowly. The town had really been exhausted of its most available forces. And it was owing to the fact that so much of our young blood had been absorbed into the other regiments that we were represented in the 146th by only about 20 men, and that five of those averaged over 45 years of age.

Other towns in the county that had not before been reached by the high tide of patriotism, responded freely to the call, some of them raising nearly complete companies.

Students and professional men also felt the impulse. On the roster of the 146th were twelve to fifteen college men–three clergymen, two theological students, and a large number of well-educated teachers and citizens. This large admixture gave a character to the regiment that it kept to the end. Its military character will be spoken of in another piece. The first nucleus of a regiment, its gathering point, is in its Adjutant. The formative life of a regiment is entirely one of record–the enrollment of its members–their assignment to companies–dates of enlistment–residence–age–personal description–transfers from one company to another–really a personal history of every man from the time he first joins the regiment.

And when the regiment machinery is all in motion, and the body of men become incorporated with the army, the Adjutants' office continues the record of that personal history with every morning roll call. Every absence, with leave, or without leave, every detail for detached duty, every sickness in hospital, every departure from or return to the regiment, every breach of discipline or order, every punishment--all is recorded in the Adjutant's books.

This detail of organization was natural and easy to the well-trained mind of our friend, who assumed its duties in August, 1862, on the grounds of Camp Huntington, at Rome, immediately after the departure of the 117th from those grounds.

Indeed, I think he began his labors there some days before the 117th left. He felt a great interest in the formation of the 146th, and his work on his papers and books often continued far into the night. As the organization progressed, of course active work began in other departments, and employed many other busy heads and hands. But the initiatory work was almost wholly his.

When Col. Garrard arrived at Rome to take command of the regiment, his complete knowledge of military matters, and twelve years of practical service, helped things along wonderfully. The routine duties of the regiment in all its departments went on smoothly, rapidly and correctly, and so they continued as long as the organization lasted.

The final settlement of its affairs was easily and promptly made, in consequence of his intelligent direction and supervision of its daily routine. The faithful work of Adjutant Jenkins won the esteem of Col. Garrard, and he soon desired to transfer his activity and enthusiasm from the record of the men, to the drilling and handling of the men themselves. In accordance with his wishes, he was promoted to Major, and then to Lieutenant Colonel before leaving Rome.

In his new position he exhibited the same interest and industry. But during the camp at Rome not much of drilling could be done, while enlistment, equipment and company formations were going on all the time.

On Saturday morning, October 10$^{th}$, 1862, the 146$^{th}$ left Rome, and on the afternoon of Tuesday, the 13$^{th}$, reached its camping ground just back of Arlington Heights, across the Potomac from Washington. That night was its first bivouac, for none of the camp equipage was on the ground, and many had not even a blanket. The discomfort of that first night under the stars was for long afterwards a subject of laughter and derision when in the face of far greater trial and distress.

Of that month of preparation at Camp Seward, not much is to be said, except that during it were laid the foundations of the excellent military character afterward exhibited by the regiment. It was a month of earnest study in books, of tactics, in the manual of arms, in field movements, and in the methods of camp living. The soldier must go through an acclimation, a seasoning of his body to the new requirements of his changed food and lodging, fully as necessary to his efficiency as a familiarity with arms and movements.

Those who imagine camp life in the intervals of campaigns, in a disciplined regiment, to be one of ease and idleness, would be astonished at the time devoted to hard work.

Col. Garrard was too experienced a soldier to take a green regiment directly into the field for service, as so many were taken. He knew the wants of new men, and their capacity to endure.

Of course Col. Garrard was the moving spirit in the training of the regiment, and he was warmly seconded by many of his subordinates. But among those subordinates Lieut. Col. Jenkins was pre-eminent for his zeal and hard work; and this zeal never for a moment intermitted, to the day of his death.

Thus was the regiment gradually inured to the hardships of the life before it. Like the bivouac of the first night at Camp Seward, what was at the time thought of the daily routine of the mouth there, was duly revised, in the light of subsequent trials, when the comforts and luxuries of the camp were remembered with an astonishment that soldiers could ever have had such.

On the 9th November, 1862, the 146th left Camp Seward, and on the 13th reached and joined the Army of the Potomac at Warrenton. To show one of the processes of curtailing its luxuries, it may be mentioned that the ten four-horse and six-mule army teams and wagons that were then required to transport its baggage and camp equipage were soon reduced to seven, then to five, then to three, and finally to two; and during active campaigns the visits of those left were like those of angels, "far between."

When the regiment became absorbed into the Army of the Potomac it formed part of the Third Brigade of the Second Division of the Fifth Corps, Gen. Hooker commanding. The other regiments of the brigade were the 5th N. Y. (Duryea's Zouaves) and the 140th N. Y., whose Colonel, O'Rorke, was a West Point classmate of Col. Garrard, and also was Gen. Warren commanding the brigade. The division was well known as Sykes' division of regulars. The other two brigades of it were composed entirely of regulars, and these were all the regulars in the Army of the Potomac. Thus the division became permeated with the spirit and discipline that pertain to the regular army.

By "discipline" is meant its primary sense of "to learn," not simply the discipline that prescribes military salutes, habits of address, length of hair and polish of shoes, or punishment for offences, but the discipline that makes perfect in the manual of arms, the movements in the field, the prompt and cheerful obedience to orders, the unflinching

**GOUVERNEUR KEMBLE WARREN**

Warren was born at Cold Springs, New York, on January 8, 1830. He entered Military Academy at West Point at age sixteen and graduated second in his class, then served as a topographical engineer until the beginning of the Civil War. He commanded the 5th New York Infantry, and later the brigade and corps (Fifth) in which the 146th New York served. For his heroic actions at Gettysburg, he became known as "the Savior of Little Round Top"–the key to the Union position. He died on August 8, 1888, at Newport, Rhode Island. His brother, Robert Parrott Warren, seved as an officer in the 146th. (Patrick A. Schroeder Collection)

endurance and courage that face forced marches, the ballet and the bayonet of the foe, even death itself, without wavering.

These qualities come to masses of men only by earnest, systematic work and long continued practice. Scattered individuals seem to possess them almost by intuition, and the labor is theirs to imbue their comrades with their own spirit. This was conspicuously the labor of David T Jenkins.

Although spare of habit, and not robust in constitution, his almost unfailing good health enabled him to do much hard work and undergo with safety many hardships. The only serious illness now remembered was while on the first march of the regiment from Camp Seward to join the army. He had symptoms of fever for a day or two, and gradually grew worse until on the forenoon of the fourth day's march he gave out near Gainesville, about ten miles from Warrenton, then Gen. Sigel's headquarters. Two of his companions had leave to fall out of the ranks long enough to find a place for him and his horse. A family was found willing to give him a room and bed. A portion of the best the mess contained was left, with a faithful colored servant of the mess to wait on him, who disappeared the next day and the provisions with him. A requisition on Gen. Sigel's quartermaster produced a supply of forage for his horse.

This was all that could be done, and he was left to himself among strangers. It is one of the hardships of moving army life that the exigencies of the service seldom admit even such slight attention as this to a comrade who is dropped from the ranks by illness of by bullet. While at Gainesville he was pleasantly surprised by a visit from his brother, Capt. Jas. E. Jenkins, who was with the army at Warrenton.

The Army of the Potomac was again in motion on the 17$^{th}$ November, and after two or three days' march went into camp near Fredericksburg. On the 29$^{th}$ November Col. Jenkins rejoined the regiment, still this and pale from his fever. He grew too ill at Gainesville to remain with safety and went to Washington, where two friendly Vernon boys, J. J. Knox, present Controller of the Currency, and W. Pitt Sherman, then in one of the Auditor's rooms at the Treasury Department, found comfortable quarters for him.

On the day that the 146$^{th}$ left Camp Seward to join the Army of the Potomac, Gen. McClellan was relieved of its command, and was

Quarters of 146th Regt., N. Y. S. Vols., at Camp Seward near Washington, D. C.

Taken from the back of an old envelope

succeeded by Gen. Burnside. After a camp of about two weeks near Fredericksburg, the regiment was aroused at early dawn of December 19th by the roar of artillery at the front of the line on the Rappahannock, some three or four miles distant.

These sounds, afterwards so fearfully familiar, were the first tokens of actual conflict heard by the 146th, and officers and men threw up their caps and shouted with enthusiasm over the prospect of a fight or anything else that would break up the monotony of camp life. But after one or two battles such sounds had a different effect, and camp life seemed more attractive than it formerly did. The cannonading heard that morning was the opening of the battle of Fredericksburg. It was to dislodge the rifleman sheltered by the buildings and fences in the city, who by their fire prevented the laying of pontoons on which to cross the river.

Another month of camp life brought the army to what has gone into history as Burnside's "Mud March."

On the morning of January 20th, 1863, they started for the upper fords of the Rapidan, the south fork of the Rappahannock, the two rivers then dividing the two armies. It was a fine, sunny, frosty morning, with the ground dry and smooth, but that evening began a terrible storm of rain, snow and sleet that produced a mud of such phenomenal depth and tenacity that it gave its name to the movement, and became pre-eminent over all other Virginia muds, where distinction of that kind seemed impossible. The march was continued through the night, in order to keep the movement hid from the enemy, at points where the road ran near the river.

Of course the continuous passage of infantry, cavalry, artillery and heavy pontoon trains before morning made the way absolutely impassable.

For the third time the men went to the old camp ground, and again rebuilt their camp. But it was many days–perhaps weeks–before all of the artillery and pontoons were removed from the mire.

Although the discomforts and hardships of that march were terrible, there was after all so much that was ludicrous in it that a smile or a guffaw generally went with the shrug with which it was afterwards spoken of.

**ROBERT J. SELKIRK**

Selkirk wears the zouave uniform of the 5th New York Infantry that the officers of the 146th wanted to emulate. He was born at Bethleham, NY, in 1832. At age 28, while working as a clerk, he enlisted as a private in Co. E of the 5th New York, Duryée's Zouaves, on July 17, 1861. He was 5'7 7/8", had a sandy complexion, gray eyes, light hair, and had been employed as a clerk. Selkirk was detailed as Division Postmaster on Dec. 3, 1862; and then was assigned duty as Post Office Agent in Washington, DC, on March 23, 1863. There he was in charge of supervising mail carriers to Aquia Creek; VA, where the Army of the Potomac was encamped. He, along with the three-year men of the 5th New York, was transferred to the 146th New York on May 4, 1863, where he was assigned to Co. D. Selkirk was again appointed Division Postmaster in August 1863. He evidently enjoyed his duties and the service as he re-enlisted as a veteran volunteer on March 21, 1864. Apparently while on his veterans' furlough, Selkirk married Isabella Shick while home in New York City on March 16, 1864. He mustered out of service at Syracuse, NY, on July 26, 1865. Selkirk died at 1216 5th St., NW, Washington, DC, on May 12, 1875, and was buried at Graceland Cemetery in Washington, DC. (Patrick A. Schroeder Collection)

That ended the winter's campaigning. Recitations and discussions of tactics, regimental and field drill target firing, filled up the time.

About the 1st March, '63, Capt. James E. Jenkins, a brother of the Colonel, was transferred to the 146th from Mann's Company of Calvary, which had been serving as body guard with McClellan, Burnside, and then with Hooker, who had succeeded Burnside in the command of the Army of the Potomac on the 27th January, '63. The two brothers had been within visiting distance most of the time since the 146th joined the army, but both longed for a closer companionship. Besides, several college chums and many other friends of Capt. Jenkins were in the 146th. At this time, too, short furloughs were granted, and for a few days the widow at Vernon again saw her first born, and home companions again took him by the hand.

On his return to camp near Potomac Creek the officers of the Regiment discussed the project of making it a zouave regiment. The 5th N. Y., Duryea's Zouaves, wore the costume of the French Zouaves, red fez cap, dark blue open jacket, red baggy trousers and leather leggings. They were very proficient in the zouave drill and bayonet exercise.

The easy and graceful movements of men thus dressed and drilled were conspicuous, and their nonchalant swing on a march could be discerned as far as the men could be seen. It was soon decided to adopt the costume and drill. The department officers at Washington were ready to grant any request of Col. Garrard's, and the clothes were at once ordered to be made in Philadelphia. They had previous to this, at his request, sent out to the regiment new Springfield muskets in the place of the very poor Austrian guns that had been supplied in New York. The uniforms ordered retained the red fez and leather gaiters, but the short open jacket and baggy breeches were both of the common light army blue color. They were not received fro some time, but the drill was immediately, and in large doses. For an hour or two before breakfast on those clear, frosty mornings every officer in the regiment, both staff and line, was on the parade ground with a musket and bayonet, undergoing practice in lunge, thrust, parry and guard, until the beads of perspiration came thick and fast.

With April came rumors of movements that died away as they came. Sunday night, the 26th, the boys went to bed without a suspicion that the general call would be sounded at 5 A. M. the next morning, with orders to march at 10 A. M.

At 9:30 A. M. Sykes' Division was in line, and at 10 left the ground that many of them were never to see again. The Quartermaster of the 146th was in despair over a vast pile of tents and camp equipage left on the ground which there was no transportation, but which could not be abandoned without orders. After a delay of some hours an order was obtained from the Division Commander to burn them.

So many movements of the army had been betrayed to the enemy by premature notices of preparation that only the higher field officers knew the plans.

It is of the daily surprises to the rank and file and lower officers of an army in motion, to start every morning on a new journey, without knowing whether they are go east or west, north or south, through forests or open fields, or how far they will go, until the trumpet sounds the welcome halt for the night, unless perchance a quicker summons comes from that power which is greater that of any man, and whose order supercedes the order of the highest General.

The morning of the third day brought them to the Rappahannock at Kelly's Ford, which was crossed on pontoons, and at night they reached the Rapidan at Ely's Ford. There being no pontoons here, they were compelled to wade, the water being waist deep. It was dark before the crossing was completed and they slept on the river bank, not liking the make up of the river bed.

There were now on rebel ground, and at daylight moved rapidly to the rear of United States ford on the Rappahannock, near its junction with the Rapidan, in hopes to capture a rebel force and battery guarding that ford. The men escaped, but the guns were captured. They were now on the ground that was to become so famous in the history of the army–that of Chancellorsville and the Wilderness. The movement from United States ford was towards Fredericksburg and parallel with the river. That night (30th April) found them near rebel lines. A short advance of Sykes' Division the next morning (May 1st) brought them within the rebel lines without the flank support that had been expected. Then began that terrible, blind, running, bush fight that continued for four days, with alternating success and defeat. When Sykes' Division was likely to be surrounded, a retreat was ordered, but the troops were so scattered and isolated by the dense growth of scrub that fills the region that Companies A and G of the 146th did not hear the recall and kept on. They were soon in the midst of Stonewall Jackson's corps, and about twenty were killed and thirty taken prisoners. Among the latter were Capt. Joseph Durkee, of Augusta, and Lieut. Matteson, of Rome.

Capt. Durkee had a army badly shattered, and was taken to Jackson's headquarters, where it was amputated by surgeon Todd of the rebel force, a half-brother of Mrs. Lincoln. The next day Stonewall Jackson himself was brought in on the shoulders of his men, mortally wounded.

On May 5th this drawn battle was abandoned by Gen. Hooker, who recrossed the Rappahannock with a loss of over 17,000 men. The rebel loss is estimated at 18,000.

And now May 6th saw Sykes' Division again and for the last time on its old camping ground, between Potomac Creek and the Rappahannock, about three miles from Fredericksburg.

Again was the camp rebuilt and the situation made as comfortable as possible–for it is the old soldier's practice to build a camp as if he expected to stay in it a year. The Fifth New York (Duryea's Zouaves) was originally a two years' regiment, but the recruits added to it were three years' men. The time of the two years' men expired during the Chancellorsville fight, but they would not, of course, forsake their comrades at such a time. As soon as the Rappahannock was recrossed the two years' men were mustered out, and the three years' men transferred to the 146–334 of them. They were not strangers, for they had camped, marched and fought together for six months.

Nearly a month more in camp routine, when, on June 1st, the long-expected new zouave uniform was received and distributed. It was also pay day, which is always a busy one. So midnight found many of the men still up, and at that hour came an order to march at 4 that morning. These early morning calls were becoming disagreeable.

The new uniforms were donned, surplus clothing and camp equipage packed up and started for Washington, and at 4 A. M. the regiment was again on the road, and homeless. Their designation now was Richard's ford, about 15 miles up the Rappahannock, near where the Rapidan joins it.

The rebels had made demonstrations of crossing, and the 146th

**JOHN EDWIN NEWMAN**

Curiously, in this photograph, Newman has no leggings, only socks under his jambiéres. He originally enlisted as a corporal in Co. D of the 5th New York Infantry on July 8, 1861. Newman was 29 years old, stood 5'9", had a dark complexion, gray eyes, fair hair, was employed as a carpenter and had been born at Stamford, CT. He was reduced to the ranks for disobedience to orders, then was detailed at his trade of carpenter. Newman was wounded at the Battle of Second Manassas, VA, on Aug. 30, 1862. He deserted from the hospital, but returned to the ranks in Apr. 1863. Transferred with the other 234 three-year men present in the field on May 9, 1863, Newman joined Co. A of the 146th, and was promoted corporal in Nov./Dec. 1863. Newman took sick on May 5, 1864. He rejoined the regiment in time to be wounded in the right foot during the June 18, 1864, assault on Petersburg. The bullet struck his foot cutting the skin "under the planta perdis and making its exit in a horizontal line without injuring the bone." Sent to the Second Division Hospital in Alexandria and admitted there on July 4. Newman was discharged from the hospital for the expiration of his term of service on July 18, 1864. (Brian C. Pohanka Collection)

was to act as a picket guard for about three miles of river. The camps were in the dense woods along the high river bank, while the rebel pickets occupied the opposite wooded bank. The river is narrow there, and friendly talk went over it daily. The officers were frequently saluted from rebeldom, and of course returned the courtesy.

When the new uniforms of the 146$^{th}$ first appeared upon the river bank, the neighbors on the other side were nonplused. Soon a group of rebel officers was seen, field glass in hand, examining the new comers. The costume was zouave in cut, and the fez was the same, but the short open jacket and baggy breeches were light blue instead of the dark blue jacket and red breeches of the old zouaves. Finally a rebel picket on the river's edge shouted over–"We know who you uns be! You'm the old reg-legs in new clothes!"

They had hit it right the first time–for they had several times faced the "red-legs," as they called Duryea's Zouaves, in battle. This camp was on the whole a very pleasant one, the regiment being for the time an independent command. During a part of the time Col. Garrard was in command of the brigade, so that Col. Jenkins was left in command of the regiment. The instructions were to keep watch of the river with the utmost vigilance, day and night, for some movement of the rebels was in progress. After a few days our pickets noticed that while the water of the Rappahannock came down clear, that of the Rapidan came muddy, with no indication of there having been a storm. This continuing the next day, it was reported to regimental headquarters, and from thence up.

It proved to be one of the first indications of the real purposes of the rebel army. The Rapidan flows through a region then occupied entirely by the rebels, and their long trains of wagons and artillery and troops of cavalry were crossing its waters miles above its junction with the Rappahannock, where the 146$^{th}$ was stationed, and the tell-tale mud came down and told the story. Lee had started for Pennsylvania. It was therefore necessary that our army should keep between him and Washington. On the 14$^{th}$ June the 146$^{th}$ left Richards' ford, following up the line of the Orange & Alexandria Railway towards Washington. The route led through Brentsville to Manassas Junction, which was reached on the 15$^{th}$.

**ALBERT ROSS**

Here, Ross wears his 5th New York jacket with the pantaloons of the 146th New York. He was born in New York City on July 4, 1843. At age 19 he enlisted in the 5th New York Infantry, and had previously been employed as a steward. Ross had hazel eyes, dark brown hair, a dark complexion, and stood 5'93/4". Present at the battle of Chancellorsville. He was transferred from Co. A of the 5th New York to Co. K of the 146th on May 4, 1863. Ross sprained his arm and ankle on June 22, 1863, and never returned to duty with the regiment in the field. In Jan./Feb. 1864 he was posted at the "Rendezvous of Distribution, Va" being detailed in the kitchen. Another accident befell Ross on May 11, 1864, when he toppled from a horse and this time injured his hand and arm. He was discharged June 3, 1865. Ross married Maria Josephine Obider on Nov. 9, 1865. He died at age 82 at 312 Decatur Street in Brooklyn on Aug. 2, 1925. (Brian C. Pohanka Collection)

This march of 40 miles was during two intensely hot days, with constant clouds of dust enveloping the panting men and horses. More than half of the regiment was left straggling behind, many so prostrated with heat and fatigue that they never fully recovered from it. Besides, water was very scarce on the route, and man and beast drank eagerly from stagnant puddles thick with mud. What was the exigency that demanded such a forced march, they never knew.

A rest of two days was imperative, and then the march was renewed, through Centreville and Bull Run to Aldie, which was reached on the 19th June. This is a pleasant little town among the Bull Run mountains, an outlying range of the Alleghenies. Here the air was pure and cool, and as rebel cavalry were encountered near here and had a hard fight with ours under Buford, they remained seven days.

The 146th and the 155th Pennsylvania were sent through Aldie Pass into Loudon valley and formed a picket line of about three miles. This region had not been so devastated as that left behind; wild cherries abounded, and even pigs and chickens were not unknown. This stop was always remembered with pleasure. Near the camp was Oak Hill Mansion, the home of President Monroe.

On the 26th the army moved again, passing through Leesburg, crossing the Potomac at Edward's Ferry, and the Monacacy near Buckeytown, camping near Frederick City.

On June 28th Gen. Hooker was superseded in the command of the Army of the Potomac by Gen. Meade. This left the command of the Fifth Corps with Gen. Sykes, while Gen. Ayres had the Second Division and Gen. Weed the Third Brigade, in which was the 146th. On June 29th the army moved north again, through Middleburg and Taneytown, reaching Hanover, about 12 miles from Gettysburg, on July 1st. Here the streets were littered with dead rebel cavalry horses killed the day before, and the guns of the First and Eleventh Corps already boomed in the distance from Gettysburg, and Gen. Reynolds, their gallant commander, lay dead on the field. His encounter with the rebels at that particular point was entirely accidental, and neither Meade or Lee chose the ground, or were present at the first day's fight. The Fifth Corps marched all night, and reached the battle-field, which was rapidly covering a line of over six miles, at early dawn. The Fifth and Sixth Corps were held in reserved and did not fighting until afternoon. Gen. Sickles Third Corps

**GEORGE GORDON MEADE**

Born in 1815, Meade entered West Point in 1831. He later served in the Topographical Engineers, and in the Mexican War. A Pennsylvanian, he received promotion to Brigadier General in 1861 and took charge of three brigades from that state. Steady and reliable, but known to have a bad temper, Meade took command of the Army of the Potomac just prior to the Battle of Gettysburg, where he defeated Lee and the Army of Northern Virginia. He led the Army of the Potomac for the rest of the war. Meade died November 6, 1872, from pneumonia, and was buried at Laurel Hill Cemetery in Philadelphia. (Patrick A. Schroeder Collection)

were held in reserved and did no fighting until afternoon. Gen. Sickles' Third Corps occupied the extreme left our line, was flanked by a strong rebel force, badly used and in great danger. Sickles had lost his leg. The Second Brigade of regulars of the Second Division, Fifth Corps, was sent in to help Sickles, and it was hard pressed, losing 500 men out of 800 in half an hour.

Then the Third Brigade was sent in, the 146$^{th}$ leading. Just as they had reached the conflict and halted to deliver their fire, Gen. Warren Meade's Chief of Staff, came rushing down the steep sides of Little Round Top hill, still farther to the left, and ordered the brigade to charge and take it, as it was being occupied by the rebels and would flank our whole line. With cheers, up scrambled the boys, under a galling fire, over and among the great bare boulders that covered the hill, met the rebels on the top, and in ten minutes drove them down the opposite slope and kept them down. In less than half an hour they had four 30-pound Parrott guns in position and doing splendid work, and before the next morning eight more. A rough stone wall was soon made on the side fronting the rebels, which gave them much shelter.

This ended the second day's fight, and that part of the field was tolerably quiet until noon of July 3$^{rd}$. Fighting had been going on nearly all night in a distant part of the line. Soon after noon began one of the most terrific cannonading ever heard, along the whole line. Our boys well knew that this was only a prelude to closer work.

And now came the closing scenes of the great battle, when, under cover of their fire, 20,000 rebels moved swiftly out in three successive lines, each nearly three miles long, and charged across the open fields between the two armies. As they neared our lines they were met by a deadly fire, but still they pressed on, and on, until at a few points they passed into our lines, capturing guns and gunners. but they were soon shaken off, so badly shattered that the battle was ended. It closed with a thunder storm that rivaled the artillery in noise. The Third Brigade lost its commander, Gen. Weed, its battery commander, Capt. Hazlett, Col. O'Rorke of the 140$^{th}$ New York, several minor officers, and about 200 men. Col. Jenkins was standing by Gen. Weed and caught him as he fell, and had hardly laid him on the ground when Capt. Hazlett also fell at his side. Capt. Jenkins was among the badly wounded, but rejoined the regiment about six weeks after.

Colonel David T. Jenkins and Staff, when Col. Jenkins was in Command of Third Brigade, Second Division, Fifth Corps, Warrenton Junction, Va., Winter of 1864

The location of the 146th overlooked nearly the whole field of that day, and Gen. Meade from that point directed the battle. The Union loss was 23,000, the rebel loss 28,000, and 25,000 small arms were collected from the field.

By the death of Gen. Weed, Col. Garrard came in command of the brigade, and Col. Jenkins was from that time Colonel of the 146th. On the eve of July 5th the regiment left Gettysburg in the direction of Emmetsburg and South Mountain. Again they marched through the golden wheat fields of Southern Pennsylvania, the wheat in some fields reaching the shoulders of the men. Williamsport was reached on July 11th, and there the regiment had quite a skirmish with the enemy.

On July 17th the Potomac was recrossed at Berlin, and the regiment marched through Loudon valley, at the base of the Alleghenies, having several skirmishes on the way, notably at Manassas Gap. Thence to Warrenton, where they stayed about a week, and then to Beverly Ford, on the upper Rappahannock, reaching there about August 5th, where they had one of their pleasantest camps, and remained until the 16th, September, when they moved across the river and camped near Culpepper Court House.

About October 10th the regiment recrossed the river and moved to Fairfax Court House. Several moves during October left them November 1st near Warrenton Junction. The regiment spent the winter of '63-4 near this point, being scattered along several miles of the railway, which they guarded. From January 1st Col. Jenkins was in command of the brigade, from Col. Garrard's removal to Washington. January 5th to 25th he had command of the division, owing to the temporary absence of Gen. Ayres. Col. Jenkins had constructed two forts on his line of railway, that were much praised by Gen. Sykes. Capt. Jenkins with three companies of the 146th built one of them, and Lieut. Col. Curran the other. The last of February Col. Jenkins made a short visit (his last one) to his home, full of hope and promise. The joy of meeting was too quickly followed by the pain of his parting , and he was gone forever. March 8th Gen. Grant was placed in command of the whole army of the United States, though Gen. Meade still had the Army of the Potomac.

Group of Officers of 146th Regiment at Headquarters of Third Brigade, Second Div., Fifth Corps, four days before the Battle of the Wilderness. The majority of these Officers were killed or wounded in the charge at the Battle of the Wilderness on May 5, 1864

Standing, left to right—Lt. Chalmers, Lt. Loomis, Lt. York, Capt. Wilson, Capt. Stewart, Capt. Jenkins, Lt. Walker, Capt. Cushman, Lt. Timmerman, Quartermaster Egleston, Capt. B. F. Wright, Lt. King, Lt. Coan (with hat), Lt. Lowery, Lt. Fowler, Lt. Sweet (with cloak), Lt. Fitzpatrick, Capt. Durkee

Sitting, left to right—Asst. Surgeon Fenwick, Capt. Henry Jones, Surgeon Flandrau, Col. David T. Jenkins, Major Grindlay, Lt.-Col. Curran, Adjutant Wright, Chaplain Payson

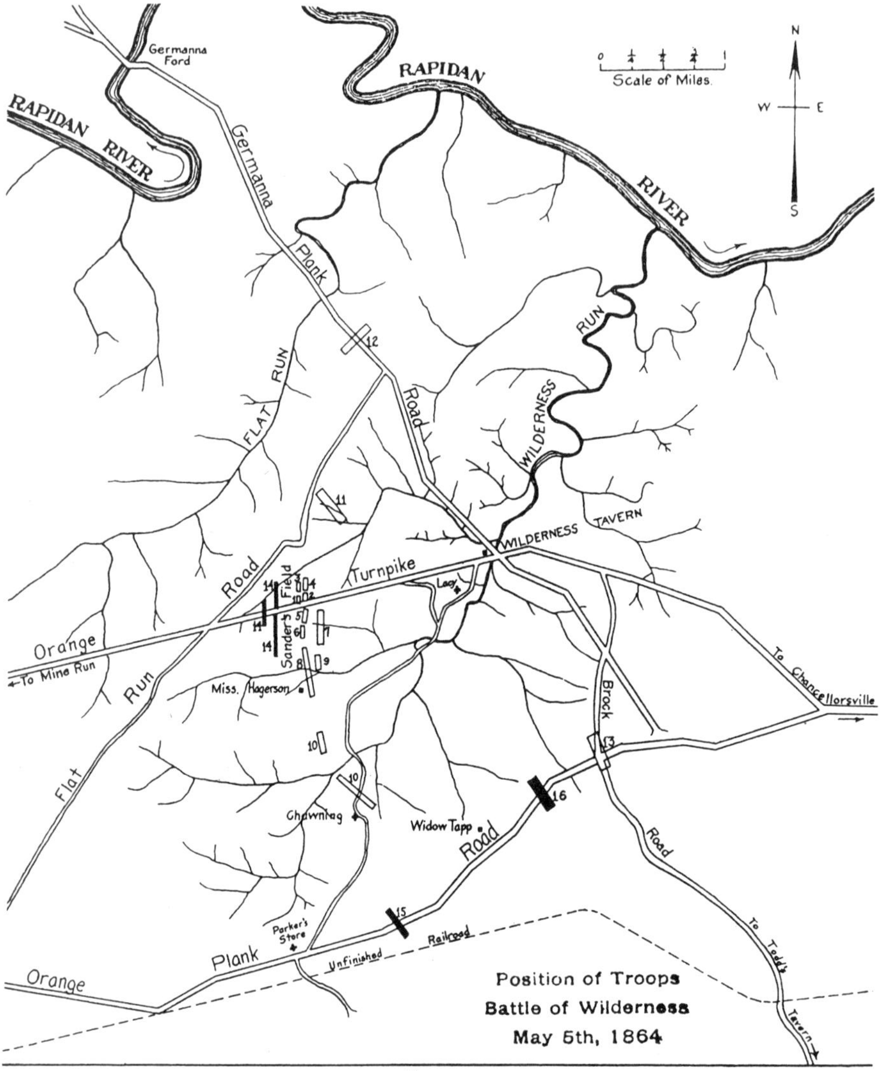


-UNION
-CONFEDERATE

GRIFFIN'S DIVISION

AYRES' BRIGADE
1– 140th NEW YORK
2– 146th NEW YORK
3– U.S. REGULARS
4– 91st AND 155th PENNSYLVANIA
5– BARTLETT'S BRIGADE
6– SWEITZER'S BRIGADE

7– ROBINSON'S DIVISION
8– WADSWORTH'S DIVISION
9– MARYLAND BRIGADE
10–CRAWFORD'S DIVISION

11– WRIGHT'S DIVISION, 6th CORPS.
12– RICKETT'S DIVISION, 6th CORPS.
13– GETTY'S DIVISION, 6th CORPS.
14– EWELL'S CORPS OF CONFEDERATES.
15– WILCOX'S DIVISION OF CONFEDERATES.
16– HETH'S DIVISION OF CONFEDERATES.

About April 1st that army was reorganized, its five corps reduced to three, viz: Hancock's Second, Warren's Fifth, and Sedgwick's Sixth. After the Rapidan was crossed, Burnside's Ninth was added. The 146th was now brigaded with three other zouave and the five regular regiments. Gen. Ayers had the brigade and Gen. Griffin the division.

May 3rd, '64, the army again started, the Fifth Corps crossing the Rapidan at Germania Ford May 4th, and it again stood on the old familiar ground they had left after the Chancellorsville fight, precisely one year before.

On the morning of May 5th they found the Wilderness woods in front of them filled with rebels and prepared at once to attack them. During the forenoon Co. Jenkins was in command of the line of the division pickets, but learning that an attack was to be made after noon, he asked to be returned to his regiment, that he might lead it. In the afternoon the 146th and the 140th were directed to attack. They did so, and were received with such a terrific fire that but few of them got near the rebel lines, and these were either killed or taken prisoners. They were to have been supported by two Pennsylvania regiments, one on each flank. These failed to come in time, and they were immediately flanked at both wings by the rebels. Col. Curran was shot through the heart and instantly killed. The last that was ever seen of Col. Jenkins he stood with his back against a tree, leaning on his sword, a bullet wound in his body and another in his head, and calling to his men to "go on."

Thus, in less than ten minutes, was almost annihilated as brave a regiment as ever fought. The 146th lost 14 out of 24 officers, and 342 men out of 556.

Many other regiments were just as brave–none more so. Many other commanders were just as brave and patriotic as the Colonel of the 146th–none more so. As soon as the ground could be visited in safety, the friends of Col. Jenkins and Lieut. Col. Curran made several extended researches for their bodies, but they were never found. His neck scarf and pocket-knife, from a rebel private, prisoner at Elmira, and his watch, from a rebel officer, prisoner at Fort Delaware, were the only tokens of Col. Jenkins ever obtained.

His character as a citizen, from boyhood to manhood, is known to you all. His character as an officer, with an important command, is only known to his military associates. Enthusiastic in everything

**A. PIERSON CASE**

At 44 years old, the gray bearded Case was one of the eldest officers with the regiment, being mustered in as a first lieutenant and regimental quartermaster on Aug. 30, 1862. The firing of Hazlett's battery over the heads of the regiment during the Battle of Gettysburg on July 3, 1863, led Case to comment that it seemed "as if the end of the world had come." On Oct. 25, 1863, he tendered his resignation on account of "physical infirmities" (diarrhea and severe gastric complications) limiting the performance of his duties. Colonel Jenkins and Brig. Gen. Garrard, regretted the loss of this officer, but endorsed his resignation which was accepted two days later. Case was of rather distinguished personage. Born in Vernon on Mar. 22, 1818, he had married Lovina W. Coburn of Homer on May 30, 1839. Case served a term in the New York State Legislature in 1852. He was appointed Cashier of the Bank of Vernon in 1879, and in 1893, became the bank's president. Case died Sept. 15, 1900, at Vernon. Not only was Case a comrade, he was a friend and admirer of the Jenkin's brothers, and penned most of this memorial book. (Dept. of Mil. & Naval Affairs, NY State Adjt. Gen. Office, Albany, NY)

pertaining to the perfection of his command–indefatigable in his labors to promote its efficiency–he aimed always at the best–the highest.

Impatient at times of what seemed to him like needless contradiction, or opposition, he pursued his plans for the good of the regiment with wonderful tenacity and patience.

In a time of heroes, he too was a hero–he was ours, and we ought to be proud of him.

*Maj. A. P. Case*

**AN UNIDENTIFIED 146th NEW YORK ZOUAVE**

This corporal poses for his photograph during the regiment's 1863-64 winter encampment. (Patrick A. Schroeder Collection)

Group of Officers of 146th Regt. at Warrenton Junction, Spring of 1864

# IDENTIFICATION CHART OF OFFICERS OF 146TH NEW YORK REGIMENT

RANK · GIVEN · AS · OF · APRIL · 15 · 1864

1. CAPT · B · F · WRIGHT ·
2. 2ND LIEUT · A · E · BROWNELL ·
3. 1ST LIEUT · A · I · KING ·
4. ASSIST · SURGEON · ROBT · FENWICK ·
5. 1ST LIEUT · LEVI · H · YORK ·
6. 1ST LIEUT · Q'T'M'R · MARVIN · EGGLESTON ·
7. CAPT · THOMAS · WILSON ·
8. CAPT · HENRY · E · JONES ·
9. LIEUT · COL · HENRY · H · CURRAN ·
10. CAPT · JAMES · E · JENKINS ·
11. COL · DAVID · T · JENKINS ·
12. CAPT · JAMES · GRINDLEY ·
13. SURGEON · THOMAS · M · FLANDRAU ·
14. CAPT · JOS · H · DURKEE ·
15. 1ST LIEUT · JOS · S · LOWERY ·
16. 2ND LIEUT · DAVID · TIMMERMAN ·
17. REGIMENTAL ADJUTANT · WILLIAM · WRIGHT ·
18. CAPT · JOS · B · CUSHMAN ·
19. 2ND LIEUT · PETER · D · FROLEIGH ·
20. 1ST LIEUT · W · H · SEWARD · SWEET ·
21. 2ND LIEUT · CHAS · L · BUCKINGHAM ·
22. PRIVATE · FROM "CO · "I" (NAME · LOST) ·
23. 2ND LIEUT · LAWERENCE · FITZPATRICK ·
24. 2ND LIEUT · ARTHUR · V · COAN ·
25. 1ST LIEUT · WILLIAM · FOWLER ·
26. 2ND LIEUT · HUGH · CHALMERS ·

**JAMES EDGAR JENKINS**

Born in Vernon on June 22, 1842, Jenkins was a student at Hamilton College at the commencement of the war. He left school along with Henry H. Curran and Charles K. Dutton, who both later served in the 146th, and helped his friends recruit 150 men at their own expense and traveled to New York City with the contingent. Unable to merge the group with another organization, the volunteers disbanded. Jenkins then assisted in raising an independent company that became known as the Oneida Cavalry. This unit had the distinguished honor of being posted to the headquarters of the Army of the Potomac, where it provided couriers and performed escort and guard duty. Jenkins enrolled as first lieutenant on Aug. 17, 1861, and mustered in Sept. 4, 1861, second in command to Captain Daniel P. Mann. He was discharged from the outfit on Mar. 1, 1863, for promotion to captain in his brother's regiment—the 146th. (Ann H. Ford Collection)

# SKETCH OF THE LIFE

## -OF--

# James E. Jenkins

---

General James E. Jenkins, who died in Vernon, N. Y., Sept. 14th, 1888, was born there in 1842. There all his early life was passed. He was a student in Hamilton College when the war broke out, and in June, 1861, he, with Henry H. Curran, Charles K. Dutton, Rush P. Cady and A. U. Bradbury, left college to raise a company of volunteers of Sickles' Brigade, then being formed in New York. Jenkins was to be Captain of the company, and Curran, First Lieutenant.

Recruiting was done in Utica, Troy, and Hudson, and before the end of June they had taken more than one hundred and fifty men to New York. Sickles was in Washington trying to get government subsistence for his men, so the new recruits could not be mustered into service and held, nor subsisted, except at the expense of those who took them there.

After losing many of them, they accepted an offer to join John Cochrane's Regiment in New York, with a direct promise that the company should retain its own officers. These promises were not kept. The men were neither mustered in, nor subsisted, and continually melted away, until they arranged to join Colonel Baker's California Regiment at Ft. Schuyler, near New York. On reaching this point, they found that Colonel Baker's regiment had suddenly received orders to remove to Washington, and had gone. Thus they were foiled in all their efforts to enter the service, and the men were scattered, after an expenditure of

**HENRY H. CURRAN**

Perhaps the most dashing and promising soldier in the regiment, only 21 years old, Curran left his studies at Hamilton College and was enrolled as first lieutenant of Co. E on Sept. 9, 1862, at Rome. He was quickly promoted to captain of Co. I on Dec. 10, 1862, and transferred to Co. B on Nov. 1, 1863. He was on detached service at Elmira Prison Camp from July 22 to Dec. 5, 1863. Curran was granted leave in Mar. 1864 and present with the regiment in Apr. as acting major. He was killed instantly May 5, 1864, at the Battle of the Wilderness. During the engagement the regiment had already suffered many casualties and was pushing through the underbrush and trees in front of the Confederate works. Lieutenant Alonzo King shouted to Curran: "This is awful!" Turning to Curran he questioned: "Where are all our men?" Curran responded: "Dead." Then a bullet struck Curran in the head. He was left on the field. Confederates rifled his body, and believed by the elaborate manner of Curran's dress that they had killed a general. His corpse was never recovered. A memorial marker was erected for him at Forest Hill Cemetery in Utica. This is the only individual photograph of Curran known and was taken by W. C. North in Utica. (Patrick A. Schroeder Collection)

over twelve hundred dollars by Jenkins and Curran and several hundred more by Dutton, Cady, and Bradbury.[1]

Curran returned to college, and Jenkins soon became interested in raising the Oneida Cavalry Company, which he joined as First Lieutenant. This was an independent command, going to the field in September, 1861. It was at once made headquarters guard for the Army of the Potomac under General McClellan, and so remained under all his successors through the war, not being mustered out until September, 1865.

In March, 1863, Lieutenant Jenkins was transferred, with the same rank, to the 146th N. Y. Infantry, known as the Fifth Oneida. This regiment was commanded by Colonel Kenner Garrard, of the regular army, its Lieutenant Colonel being David T. Jenkins, the elder brother of Lieutenant Jenkins. Thus the brothers became united again.

Lieutenant Jenkins was soon promoted to a Captaincy in the 146th, and was afterwards breveted as Major in the same regiment, for special bravery at Spotsylvania.

During the fight on Little Round Top, at Gettysburg, and very near where General Weed, Colonel O'Rorke and Captain Hazlett were killed and General Warren wounded, Captain Jenkins was shot through his neck with a musket ball, and at the same moment had his badly torn by an exploding shell.

Some pillows from a neighboring farm-house made a bed in the bottom of an ambulance, and he was thus taken to a hospital in Baltimore, accompanied by Chaplain [Albert] Erdman of the regiment. A telegram from the Chaplain at Baltimore to the Captain's mother in

---

1 In a memorial of Lieut. Colonel Henry H. Curran appears this record from the pen of Prof. North of Hamilton College:

Soon after graduation, Augustus U. Bradbury enlisted in the 128th Regt. N. Y. V., and was at once appointed Orderly, Sergeant. He died of fever in the St. James Hospital at New Orleans, Feb. 25th, 1863.

Lieut. Rush P. Cady, of the 97th N. Y. Vol., a courageous fighter because he was a devoted Christian, fell mortally wounded at Gettysburg July 1st, 1863. Major Charles K. Dutton, to whom the post of danger had a strange fascination, won rapid promotion by most undoubted merit, and was in at the death of secession. Capt. James E. Jenkins, who had been a favorite leader in college, proved himself worthy to lead, whether the result was quick death or glad victory.

Standing: Capt Wright—Lieut. Fowler
Lieut. Buckingham—Capt. Walker
Sitting: Servant—Lieut. Brownell
Capt. James Jenkins

Vernon, soon brought her there, and the wounded man soon after removed to his home in Vernon. As soon as he recovered he rejoined his command, and was an active participant in all of its movements and battles until the expiration of his three years' enlistment, in September, 1864. During this time had occurred the bloody fight of the Wilderness, May 5th, 1864, on very nearly the same ground the regiment had fought over just a year before, in the battle of Chacellorsville. In the Wilderness fight his brother, Colonel Jenkins, and Lieutenant Colonel Curran were killed and their bodies never found. The loss of the 146th in this action was fourteen officers out of twenty-four, and three hundred and forty-two enlisted men out of six hundred and fifty-four. The loss included about seventy-nine taken prisoners.

In September, 1864, Captain Jenkins re-enlisted in the Oneida Cavalry Company as its Captain, retaining this command until its muster out, in September, 1865.

Thus we have crowded into a few brief paragraphs four years of such varied and terrible experience as might well fill a life-time.

After a short stay in Vernon, Major Jenkins engaged in business in Worcester, Mass., where he married. In 1871 he removed to New York City, where he remained about ten years.

He had never recovered from the wounds and exposures of his army life, and in 1881 he was compelled to relinquish all business and seek for health.

A winter in Florida gave him no essential relief, and he seemed almost in the final stages of consumption.

A residence of a few months in Southern Dakota was very beneficial, and in 1882 he pre-empted a homestead in Brule county, near Chamberlain, removing his family there the following year.

His health seemed to improve, with some relapses, until the severe winter of 1888 brought on the attack which has ended fatally.

Although very weak and low, he had a strong desire to visit once more the home of his childhood, and if he must give up his life, to die under the roof of the old homestead, and to lie with his kindred on the hill-side.

Thus ended a brave life. Brave and manly as a boy, brave on the battle-field, brave in his last struggle with his last antagonist, death.

Capt. King—Capt. Guthrie—Lieut.
Buckingham
Servant—Capt. Cushman—Capt.
Jenkins, Petersburg, 1864

In the field he did not seem to know what fear was. Always cool and collected, a model commander, quick to see, prompt to act, he only wanted a larger field of action to have become distinguished as an officer.

Himself friendly, he always made friends, and was a favorite with his playmates, his college chums, his army comrades, and with the far Western people among who he finally cast his lot. But with his friendliness he always kept his stately, courteous manner, his self-respect, his positive, determined character, thus compelling the respect of others.

In these respects, as well as in personal appearance and dignity, he often reminded his friends of his uncle, the late Hon. Timothy Jenkins of Oneida Castle. His vigorous youth and erect form promised a long life, but four years of army hardships sapped it beyond recovery.

In 1883 Major Jenkins was elected Treasurer of Brule county, Dakota, for three years, and in 1886 was re-elected to the same office, holding it at his death.

In 1887 Governor Church appointed him Adjutant General of Dakota, and thus he became known as General Jenkins.

Had his life been spared, he gave promise of becoming one of the distinguished men in his adopted Territory. General Jenkins leaves a wife and five children in Dakota, a mother and a brother, Josiah W. Jenkins, in Vernon; and a sister, Mrs. M. P. Brewer, in Minneapolis.

Appropriate and touching funeral services were held by Rev. Dr. Calthrop of Syracuse. Comrades' hearts placed beautiful flowers around him, and comrades' hands tenderly laid away the scarred veteran who had so often led them on the field of battle.

*A. P. Case*

**JAMES EDGAR JENKINS**

Mustered in as captain of Co. H on Mar. 1, 1863, Jenkins may have soon regretted the change. Being in the thick of the fighting at Gettysburg's Little Round Top on July 2, 1863, he was twice wounded. Near the spot where Gen. Weed, Col. O'Rorke, and Gen. Warren were wounded, Jenkins was wounded in the neck, most likely by a sharpshooter's bullet. The missile passed through the back of his neck at an upward angle and exited from his mouth. Simultaneously with the bullet wound, an artillery shell exploded nearby tearing a gash in the back of the young captain. His men gathered some pillows from a nearby farmhouse and put them in the bottom of the ambulance that took him to the hospital in Baltimore. The regimental chaplain, Albert Erdman, accompanied him in the journey. The chaplain sent Jenkins' mother a telegram notifying her of Jenkins injuries. She journeyed to Baltimore and brought him home to Vernon, NY, to recuperate. Upon recovering from his injuries, he rejoined the regiment. Jenkins fought gallantly at the battles of the Wilderness, Spotsylvania, Bethesda Church, and at Petersburg, receiving the brevet rank of major in 1867 for his faithful and meritorious services. He continued with the regiment until the expiration of his term of service on Sept. 30, 1864. He was later brevetted a major for faithful and meritorious service in the 146th, to date from Mar. 13, 1865. This image was made at W. J. Baker's Studio in Utica in the spring of 1865. (Ann H. Ford Collection)

*From the Utica Daily Observer*

DEATH OF A PATRIOT SOLDIER WHO HONORED ONEIDA COUNTY

Major James E. Jenkins died yesterday at the residence of his mother in Vernon. Major Jenkins was born in Vernon, 46 years ago. He was the son of the late J. Whipple Jenkins, who ranked as one of the ablest lawyers in the State, and a nephew of Hon. Timothy Jenkins of Oneida Castle, who served with distinction as Member of Congress from his district for several years. Young Jenkins attended the schools of his native village and afterwards prepared himself for college. He entered Hamilton College and was a student there when the war broke out. He immediately left college and was one of the very first to enlist in the cause of his country. His comrades here speak of him as one of the noblest of men, truest of patriots, and bravest of soldiers. He was twice severely wounded in battle, and promoted and breveted for gallant conduct at Spotsylvania.

---

## NOTICES OF THE DEATH OF GEN. JENKINS IN DAKOTA

*From the "Brule County Democrat," Chamberlain, Dak.*

PASSED BEYOND

[Special Telegram.]–Intelligence of the death of Adjutant General James E. Jenkins, D. N. G., in Vernon, N. Y., has just been received in this city. General Jenkins has several years been threatened with consumption, and about four weeks ago left on a tour for his health over the great lakes to his old home in New York State, but he began failing rapidly from the commencement of his journey, and when he arrived in

Vernon he was in a very critical condition. Mrs. Jenkins received a telegram yesterday requesting her presence at the General's bedside at once, but before she could get ready to start another telegram arrived announcing his death. The General will be buried at Vernon, New York. General Jenkins was one of Dakota's most representative citizens. In addition to the Adjutant Generalship, he was holding the office of Treasurer of Brule county at the time of his death.

## GOV. CHURCH'S ORDER

HEADQUARTERS SECOND REGIMENT D. N.G.
GENERAL ORDERS }
No. 27 }

WATERTOWN, Dakota, Sept. 15, 1888.

**I.** The sad intelligence of the death of James E. Jenkins, Adjutant General of the Dakota National Guards, is received, filling our hearts with sorrow. To those of us who have had the pleasure of a personal acquaintance with the deceased, it is unnecessary to state that a braver soldier, a truer friend, a more honorable and courteous gentleman never lived. Suffering as he was for years, with failing health, caused by wounds received whilst defending his country's honor, he was performed all the duties of life cheerfully and without a murmur. In a position of Adjutant General of the D. N. G., he put forth his best endeavors for the benefit of the organization he loved so well, and which in turn loved him who, battle scarred and feeble from the effects of honorable wounds, was ready to do his duty towards all, at all times and under all circumstances.

His earthly warfare is over; the roll of death has summoned this gallant spirit to report for duty above, in company with his beloved commanders, McClellan, Grant and Hancock, who have preceded him. With malice towards none, he lived. Beloved and respected by all who knew him, he died. The profound sympathy of the Dakota National Guards is hereby extended to the bereaved family of the deceased, in this the hour of our common affliction. With the keenest feelings of grief at this, the time of his death, they have the consoling satisfaction of remembering with pride his unsullied life.

**II.** As a mark of respect for the memory of the deceased, it is hereby ordered that regimental headquarters, also the armory of each company, battery or troop of the Dakota National Guard be suitably draped for a period of thirty days. Also that all officers of the brigade wear the usual badges of mourning for the same period.

By order of
LOUIS H. CHURCH,
Governor and Commander-in-Chief.

MARK W. SHEAF, Colonel commanding 2nd Regiment, D. N. G.

## MEMORIAL SERVICES AT KIMBALL, DAKOTA

Sunday morning, Sept. 23, according to announcement, Reno Post, No. 35, held memorial services in their hall in honor of Past Commander James E. Jenkins. The Sons of Veterans were present in a body, and many Chamberlain friends were also there.

After some very appropriate music, the Post exercises were carried out. Gen. W. V. Lucas then made a most eloquent and touching tribute to the deceased, after which an adjournment was made to the opera hall. Here the house was closely filled, and the choir gave music to render more impressive the services. A sermon by Rev. Hubbard, of Chamberlain; scripture reading , by Rev. Furnier; remarks by C. J. Maynard, and a choice address by Major Kellam, filled the program. Adjutant Grippen read a record of the deceased.

Major Jenkins joined Reno Post as a charter member, Sept. 10th, 1883, and was elected its first Commander, which office he held with credit to himself during the early history of the Post, and by his untiring efforts in its behalf, assured its growth and success during the early years of its organization. He held his membership with Reno Post until the Great Commander gave him his final orders to cross the dark river, which he has obeyed, leaving a record of a patriotic, useful life behind him.

Both halls were decorated with flowers and emblems of mourning, and a vacant chair was draped in memory of the dead comrade. Commander C. S. Blodgett had charge of the services at the

Grand Army hall, as well as the opera house, and the services were of the most impressive character.

The following hymn was sung at the Grand Army hall:

THE GOOD DIE NOT.

With silence only as their benediction
God's angels come.
There in the shadow of a great affliction
The soul sits dumb.

Yet would we say what every heart approveth,
Our Father's will,
Calling to Him the dear ones whom He loveth
Is mercy still.

Not upon us or ours the solemn angel
Hath evil wrought;
The funeral anthem is the glad evangel;
The good die not.

God calls His loved ones, but we lose not wholly
What He has given;
They live on earth in thought and deed as truly
As in His heaven.

# REV. MR. HUBBARD'S SERMON AT THE OPERA HOUSE

"Shall you go to the war, and shall ye sit here? We will not return unto our houses until the children of Israel have inherited, every man, his inheritance."–Numbers, 32: 6-18.

When the children of Israel had completed the conquest of the country east of the Jordan, Reuben and Gad, finding Gilead and Jazes furnished good pasturage, thought to settle down there and let the other ten tribes fight their own battles. But this, Moses showed them, would be both a selfish policy and unsafe. They, convinced of the truth of what their leader urged, agreed to go on and help, in turn, their brethren in the complete conquest of Canaan.

This bit of history illustrates the though that has been uppermost in my mind since hearing to the event which is the occasion of our assembling here to-day. It is this:

The existence and prosperity of our nation to-day, as a simple fact, lays upon every citizen the obligation to lend his influence, his thought, his life, to its maintenance and perfect development. This obligation is determined in part by the necessity of our institutions to our own best welfare. We are one people as Israel was one people; our interests are identical. There are great questions of national interest, such as securing to all men the right guaranteed to them by the constitution, how to make good citizens of the immense foreign element coming to our shores; how to banish forever our national vices. These are questions which, as concerning our own interests, we ought to consider as broad minded, loyal members of a great nation. This obligation is further determined by the necessity of national prosperity to the fulfilling of our mission as a nation. Israel had a great mission upon earth, and its success in accomplishing that mission depended upon the self-sacrificing effort of the whole people. Reuben and Gad, as well as Judah and Ephraim, must contribute to the revelation of God through the people, and ultimately through one of that people–even Jesus Christ. To our nation, capable in extent of territory and abundance of resources, of maintaining the world's population, has been committed the completion of Israel's work. To us are flocking the nations of the earth. It is vain for us to try to shut them out. We ought rather to sacrifice comfort and means that in them may be formed the image of the eternal soul. But yet again, this obligation is determined by the great cost at which our present prosperity has been purchased. Our fathers fought that liberty might be established. Their sacrifices and sufferings have consecrated our very soil to liberty and manhood.

The heroes of '61 left home and business and gave their efforts and their lives to extend the privileges of liberty and more thoroughly establish the principles upon which our national institutions were founded. The terrible defeats of the early period of that war, and the dearly-bought victories of the late years, speak in saddened tones of the great price paid for liberty. Myriads of graves on Southern battle fields testify what our present prosperous condition has cost us. Houses, desolated by the demon of war, have been telling us all these years of what the mothers and fathers and wives have given, that we might live in undisturbed enjoyment of the blessings, liberty and union bring to our doors. We are reminded to-day, most forcibly, of this great price paid by our nation and its people.

There are few, I am sure, who knew Mr. Jenkins, who have not thought of the almost pathetic struggle he has maintained against the fell destroyer for years, as the result of services saving the Union. Young as he was when he came from the war, it was impossible that his hopefulness and ambition should be quenched by his disabilities, which he carried with him ever after. He would do his duty as a man and a citizen so long as he could muster strength to keep at it. When the Eastern climate threatened to cut short his career, he fled to our dryer climate, and for five years has prolonged the contest. Many of us have seen for some time that the end was nearing, and he himself felt it, yet how valiantly to the very last he struggled to fulfil his duties and a citizen and servant of the people. On the last day spent in our midst, with tired brain and trembling hand he penned the general order to the Dakota National Guard, calling their attention to the death of General Sheridan, and now his own name is added to the fast lengthening roll of the dead. This long and unequal contest comes very vividly to our minds to-day, as we recall the bent form and feeble step, but resolute eye. Let is serve to increase our veneration for our institutions. Let us in thought multiply the sacrifice of one man and one home by that of thousands, and we are not impressed with the vastness of the price our country has had to pay for the establishment of their institutions, and the freedom she offers to all?

These are momentous days upon which we are fallen. God is bringing the nations near to Himself, and He is concentrating on the forces that are to redeem the world and Himself right here in our midst. By the sacred graves on Southern battle-fields, by the shattered and weakened constitutions of the survivors, by the life which has just gone from our midst, a sacrifice to our nation's welfare, let us say with Reuben and Gad, "We will not return unto our houses until the children of Israel have inherited every man his inheritance." Men of '61, I have sometimes thought that when, in the hour of battle, your ranks thinned and you closed up the line for a fresh charge, you felt that each one must fight the harder since the line was shortened. Such a thought I would have you take with you from this sacred hour. That you and we who are younger may together bend our every energy until no foes of the Republic shall find harbor in our midst, and the man Christ Jesus shall take and mould individual and national character. Then, indeed, can it be said that our comrades have not died in vain. This broad land shall be ruled by a people every one of who is a law unto himself, and the bond that binds them shall be loyalty to duty, to country and to God.

## REQUIEM FOR THE DEAD.

Rest, soldier, rest! thy country comes,
With tender love and true,
Freely to deck thy honored bed,
Her banner o'er its turf to spread,
And on thy monument to shed
Fond memory's pearly dew.
Rest, soldier, rest! rest thou in peace.

For, at her need in days of yore,
Unswerving and sublime,
Thy fearless foot 'mid lightnings trod,
Thy life-blood fed the encrimsoned sod,
Thy prayer awoke the avenging God
To guard thy native clime.
Rest, soldier, rest! rest thou in peace.

[Sung at memorial services at Opera House.]

**JAMES EDGAR JENKINS**

Jenkins re-enlisted as captain of the Oneida Cavalry on Jan. 18, 1865, and mustered out with that company near Washington, DC, on June 13, 1865. After a short stay in Vernon, Jenkins removed to Worcester, MA, where he engaged in business. There, in 1870, he married Elizabeth Pierce. The next year, they moved to New York City and resided there about ten years. Plagued by exposure and old war wounds, Jenkins' was affected with consumption. In 1881, he gave up business and saught to restore his health; he moved to Florida, but it did little good. He and his family, now consisting of five children, then moved to Brule County, SD. The climate suited Jenkins much better, though he would have brief relapses. There he was elected the Treasurer of Brule County in 1883 and again in 1886. In 1887, Jenkins was appointed the Adjutant General of Dakota, and thus became known as "General Jenkins." The severe winter of 1888 proved fatal. Though weak, he desired to see his old home. Jenkins traveled to Vernon, NY, in 1888, where he died shortly after arriving. This photograph was taken at Claflin's Studio in Worcester, MA, on Feb. 17, 1869. (Ann H. Ford Collection)

# ADDRESS OF MAJOR A. G. KELLAM

## AT THE MEMORIAL SERVICES FOR THE LATE GEN. JAMES E. JENKINS, HELD AT KIMBALL, DAKOTA, SEPT. 23, 1888.

*Commander, Comrades and Friends:*

I regret more than I can express to you my inability to say anything worthily or properly here to-day. With very little time for reflection or premeditation, I shall be obliged to speak to you as I have written, almost at random, upon this occasion, when I feel that every thought should have been thoroughly culled and every expression carefully chosen; but I am consoled in this, that my duty to-day is not to introduce a new character to you, whose merits I must extol, whose virtues recite, and whose life I must make attractive to strangers.

The light that has just gone out, the life that has just passed to other scenes, was a familiar life to us all. While it would be a grateful office for men, and one which my personal regard for our deceased comrade would gradually lead me into, I shall attempt no eulogy upon him who is in all our hearts to-day. "We come to bury Caesar, not to praise him."

Between Major Jenkins and ourselves there was the common bond and sympathy of brotherhood. This bond and sympathy of brotherhood. This bond, friends, is not severed by death. Its chords are mystic, and stretch from shore to shore. Honoring and loving him for his virtues while living, we will now cherish his memory and cultivate the influence of his example.

Was it a mark of patriotism for a young man to leave home and college and a bright future full of budding promises, to undertake a work of danger and possibly of death, at the call of duty?–then our comrade was patriotic in his manhood.

Was it a mark of courage to discharge with unflinching fidelity every duty of the solider, through tedious camp and weary march and fiery battle?–then our comrade was brave as a soldier.

Is it a mark of honor for a man, in every place and under all circumstances, to exhibit firmly but politely the courage of his convictions?–then our comrade was a man of stainless honor.

Is it a mark of uprightness and rectitude for a citizen to pass unchallenged and uncriticized through successive terms of public office?–then our comrade was an honest man, "the noblest work of God."

Patriotism, courage, integrity, and honor. What wealth of dower to the widow! What wealth of legacy to the children!

His record as a solider was an interesting and eventful one, having actively participated in most of the battles and skirmishes of the Army of the Potomac, many of which will forever remain prominent names in the history of our country. He was breveted Major for "faithful and meritorious services" on the field, but no commission, however faithfully earned, could so fully attest his valor as a soldier, as the wounds received in battle –these cars, which were ever the constant and unimpeachable evidence of his patriotism and his courage. His experience and record as a soldier have been so recently before you that I need not now repeat the story.

Comrades, one by one we go. Link by link the chain of our brotherhood is shortening. He whom we have so often met as a comrade, is not with us to-day; with moistened eye, and quivering lip, and chastened heart, we can only *look* our love and our good-bye into the great future into which he has gone.

In all the wide universe there is nothing so mysterious as human life. The other unsolved, matchless mystery is what is *beyond* human life. These two are the supreme Arcana of time and eternity.

Our comrade has passed through the short night of unconsciousness which we call death, and has awakened in the to-morrow of the beyond. With him the mystery of death is solved. In the new life upon which his freed spirit has just entered, the may be before him unexplored fields of experience, other unsolved problems of life, other unknown futures, other great beyond. But as our faith teaches us, we love to think of him as just now starting out on a new life, unhindered by physical pains or a wasted body, inspired by new aspirations born of new knowledge, animated and strengthened by his nearer approach to greater possible achievements.

We love to think of him, as we now do, not as dead, but a just born into a new and higher life, a life in which his cherished hopes may yet ripen into fruition. A life in which he may yet fully redeem the unfulfilled promises of the present. A life constantly gladdened and made radiant by the presence of that celestial hope that always springs from the grave of a good man. Not dust to dust is it with our comrade, but from the life that now is to the life that is to come. Not into the cold and voiceless grave, but out through the portals of death only, into the widening future. Out, out, out through the darkness, beyond the mystery, into the light. What mortal man has never yet beheld is now beheld by him. Hail, thou freed spirit, and if from thy new home to-day thou caust [can] see and know us, let thy sweet spirit hover near and bless us with its benediction.

Comrades, our lights are burning low. We only sit a little longer among the waning embers of our camp-fires. We only wait a little longer for the final order of the day, "Lights out, lights out;" and when the order comes to each and all of us, may our lights, like his, go out in peace and victory. And may the new morning to which the new reveille shall awake us, be brightened with the reflected light from his side, of honorable, useful, and well spent lives; and may he, our comrade, and his loved ones, and we and our loved ones, be reunited in an everlasting brotherhood of love.

---

Gen. Jenkins' last official act before leaving Dakota was the issue of the following order on the death of Gen. Sheridan:

CHAMBERLAIN, Dakota, August 7th, 1888.

General Order No. 6.

It is with profound regret that the Commander-in-Chief is called upon to announce the death of one of the greatest soldiers of the age, General Philip H. Sheridan, who passed away on Sunday night, August 5$^{th}$, after a lingering illness of many weeks. His long days of patient suffering are ended, but the lesson of his life remains, and will form a bright page in the history of our country. Every soldier should ponder over the character of this great chieftain. From early boyhood to the culmination of his great fame he has been eager to learn, always ready for duty, obeying the orders of his superiors faithfully, and winning the confidence of all. He has been called a military genius, but this genius was made possible by his thorough knowledge and mastery of the science of war, through patient study, and to the man should the praise be ascribed. It is recorded that his commander, Gen. Grant, once questioned him as to the dispositions he had made for battle; and found the details so complete that his only order was to "go in," and he did *go in* and hurled the broken enemy in confusion from the fair valley of the Shenandoah.

It is requested that the members of the Dakota National Guard shall decorate their armories, and wear the usual badge of mourning, and take such other appropriate commemorative action as may seem to them fitting.

By order of LOUIS K. CHURCH,
Governor and Commander-in-Chief.
JAMES E. JENKINS, Adjutant General.

**THOMAS H. BROWN, JR.**

Brown was born in England on December 11, 1843. He enlisted in Company E on August 31, 1862, at Camden, when he was 18. Brown was 5'8", with a light complexion, grey eyes, light hair, and a farmer, and mustered in on October 10, 1862. From May to July he did extra duty as a Captain for Benjamin F. Wright. Brown received promotion to corporal on October 25, 1863. He was captured on May 5, 1864, at the Battle of the Wilderness, and sent to Andersonville, GA. On December 16, 1864, Brown was paroled as a prisoner of war from Charleston, SC, and was sent to Camp Parole at Annapolis, MD. On April 2, 1865, he was sent to City Point, VA, to rejoin the 146th. Brown mustered out with the regiment on July 16, 1865, near Washington, DC. In 1878, he married Ida M. Taylor in Kansas City Missouri. Brown died of pneumonia on October 30, 1930, and was buried at Elmwood Cemetery in Kansas City, Missouri. In this photo, Brown poses with a Sharps' Rifle and wears glasses. (George Picard Collection)

**HOADLY HOSFORD**

Hosford originally enlisted in Company I of the 44th New York Infantry on Sept. 17, 1861. When he enrolled he was a 21-year-old farmer who had been born in Ashland, NY. Hosford stood 5'7", with a dark complexion, brown eyes, brown hair. He was quickly promoted to corporal and made sergeant on Jan. 7, 1863. From Dec. 1863 to Apr. 1864, he was detached on recruiting duty at Albany, NY. Hosford re-enlisted as a veteran volunteer on February 19, 1864, and was transferred to Co. H of the 146th on November 2, 1864. From Aug. 18, 1864, until the end of the war he was on detached duty with the Fifth Corps' First Division Sharpshooters. Hosford mustered out with the regiment near Washington, DC, on July 16, 1865. On Sept. 16, 1864, he was commissioned a second lieutenant, but did not muster in at that rank. Here Hosford poses in a New York State jacket while a sergeant in the 44th New York Infantry. (Patrick A. Schroeder Collection)

**GEORGE H. PALMER**

A spring 1863 photo believed to be George Palmer, just before the regiment received its Zouave uniforms. He wears a frock coat with corporal chevrons. He and his brother, Alfred, both enlisted in Co. C in Utica, on Aug. 27, 1862. George was 22 years old, stood 5'4", with a light complexion, gray eyes, light hair, was born in England, and was employed as a teamster. Palmer was promoted corporal May/June 1863. He was present with the regiment until wounded in the right forearm at the Battle of the Wilderness on May 5, 1864, and sent to Stanton General Hospital in Washington, DC. He received a furlough from Stanton Hospital to home in Utica on May 17, 1864, for one month, failed to return at expiration of furlough and was listed as a deserter. Reporting to an army hospital, all charges of desertion were removed. Upon recovery of his wounds and while waiting at the Rendezvous of Distribution to be sent back to the regiment, Palmer filled the post of Henry Herbert Wood, also of the 146$^{th}$, as a mounted courier in the quartermaster's department near Washington, DC. While detailed in this work, a severe accident befell Palmer. (Patrick Schroeder Collection)

**GEORGE H. PALMER**

On Sept. 18, 1864, Palmer's horse became unmanageable, and galloped out of control and collided with the buggy of Lt. Col. Samuel McKelog—commander of the Rendezvous of Distribution camp near Alexandria, VA. McKelog was unhurt, but Palmer was thrown from his mount. McKelog related: "I came up to him, found that he was bleeding profusely from his side, there being quite a pool of blood on the ground, where he lay. . . . I had him placed in an ambulance belonging to the Commissary Department near long bridge, and taken to the hospital at Rendezvous of Distribution." Palmer suffered a severe hernia, and later had to wear a truss. He mustered out in Washington, DC, on June 2, 1865. After the war, Palmer was a milkman in Utica and kept a herd of cows. He married Sarah Allen on Dec. 6, 1865. Palmer died at 5 a.m. on Apr. 20, 1886 from a strangulated rupture or stoppage in the bowels. Affidavits in Palmer's pension file attest to his good character, noting that he "drank a glass of beer a day, but did not get intoxicated." Henry Toms recalled: "Though he was not what we would call a temperance man—sometimes he would take a glass of beer or whiskey, but I never saw him drunk . . . he could always go about his business." Palmer was interred at Forest Hill Cemetery in Utica. Palmer is splendidly attired in Zouave uniform complete with a turban wrapped around his fez. Compare with the photo on the previous page. (Michael J. McAfee Collection)

**WILLIAM A. WALKER**

This photo is believed to be Captain Walker who enrolled on Aug. 22, 1862, was 21 years old, 5'8", with gray eyes, dark hair, was born in Rome and employed as a jeweler (also given as a watchmaker). He mustered in as first sergeant of Co. B, on Oct. 10, 1862, but was returned to the ranks on Nov. 22, 1862. Walker quickly rose in rank once again being made corporal on Jan. 10, 1863, then sergeant on Feb. 1, 1863, then a second lieutenant in Co. D on Mar. 1, 1863. From May-July 1863, Walker was provost marshal for the 3rd Brigade, 2nd Division, 5th Corps and was in charge of the provost guard. Walker was transferred to Co. E on Aug. 20, 1863, then promoted first lieutenant of Co. C on Oct. 23, 1863. Given a ten-day furlough to visit his home on Dec. 12, 1863. He was shot through both arms, and captured at the Battle of the Wilderness on May 5, 1864. Confined at Staunton, VA, until being sent to Richmond on Sept. 8, then was paroled at Varina, VA, on Sept. 12 and arrived at Camp Parole, MD, two days later. Exchanged in Sept. 1864 while a paroled prisoner of war was given a 20-day leave from Camp Parole starting on Sept. 13, which was extended, as his wounds had not healed. Given a two-day furlough to visit Washington, DC, on Dec. 5, 1864, and returned to duty on Jan. 9, 1865. Walker was on special duty as the ambulance officer for the 1st Brigade, 2nd Division, 5th Corps, but returned to command the company in April. He mustered in as captain on Apr. 1, 1865. Granted leave for ten days in June to go to Rome to visit his "aged mother who is dangerously ill and not expected to recover." Walker mustered out with the regiment on July 16, 1865. Walker was made a brevet major on July 16, 1867 for "gallant and meritorious services during the war" to date from Mar. 13, 1865. He died on Dec. 18, 1911. (Donald Wisnoski Collection)

This photo of veterans of the 146th New York Infantry was taken on Oct. 11, 1920, at the Oneida County Court House in Rome, New York, during the regiment's annual reunion. Seated at the center of the photo among the veterans is Mary Genevie Green Brainard who wrote the unit's regimental history which was published in 1915. (Debbie Treiber Collection)

A group of 146$^{th}$ New York Infantry Veterans. The date and location is unknown, but among them are believed to be George Soper, Sylvester O. Cook, Frank Miller, Adison Dillenbeck, John Goodfellow, Thomas Robert, George O. Tibbetts, and Theodore Dixon. (Patrick A. Schroeder Collection)

## Announcing the *Letters Home Series* by Schroeder Publications

This series will feature letters written home by Federal soldiers of famous regiments and brigades, as well as representative letters to family members from men of Union regiments of every state. These are poignant, descriptive, and historically informative letters to loved ones. Three titles in the ***Letters Home Series*** are scheduled for release before Christmas 2001:

***Letters Home: Letters to Mother*** ISBN 1-889246-25-5

***Letters Home: Soldiers of the 20th Maine Infantry*** ISBN 1-889226-26-3

***Letters Home: The Bucktails (Pennsylvania's 42nd, 149th, and 150th Regiments)***
ISBN 1-889246-27-1

Three to five titles in this series will be released each year. Scheduled for publication in 2002 are:

***Letters Home: The Irish Brigade*** ISBN 1-889246-28-X

***Letters Home: The Iron Brigade*** ISBN 1-889246-29-8

***Letters Home: The Zouave Brigade (the 140th, 146th, and 5th Veteran New York Infantry Regiments and the 155th Pennsylvania Infantry )***
ISBN 1-88924-30-1

***Letters Home: Letters to Father*** 1-889246-32-8

With more to follow, including:

***Letters Home: The Michigan Cavalry Brigade*** ISBN 1-889246-33-6

***Letters Home: The Vermont Brigades*** (***Stannard's and the 6th Corps***)
ISBN 1-889246-34-4

***Letters Home: The Philadelphia Brigade*** ISBN 1-889246-35-2

***Letters Home: The Harvard Regiments (the 2nd and 20th Massachusetts)***
ISBN 1-889246-36-0

***Letters Home: Letters to Family and Friends*** ISBN 1-889246-37-9

***Letters Home: Letters of Battle*** ISBN 1-889246-38-7

This series will provide new, revealing, and richly informative material on the experience of the Civil War fighting men. Most books will be approximately 200 pages. Each book will contain numerous photographs, be printed in hardcover, with high quality acid free paper, and have a foreword written by Historian Brian C. Pohanka. Each volume will cost approximately $24.95 (depending on size). Subscribe to the series and receive free shipping. Subscribe now at www.civilwar-books.com or email civilwarbooks@yahoo.com or call 888-888-1865.